22 Random Photos to Draw

Welcome to the exciting world of drawing! In this activity book, you will have the opportunity to draw pictures from a variety of random photographs. Whether you are an experienced artist looking to refine your skills, or a beginner seeking a fun and relaxing way to explore your creativity, this book is the perfect choice for you. Each page contains a high-quality photograph, along with ample space for you to recreate the image through your own drawings. You will have the chance to practice drawing a wide range of subjects, including landscapes, cityscapes, portraits, and more. So grab your pencils and let's get started on this exciting artistic journey!

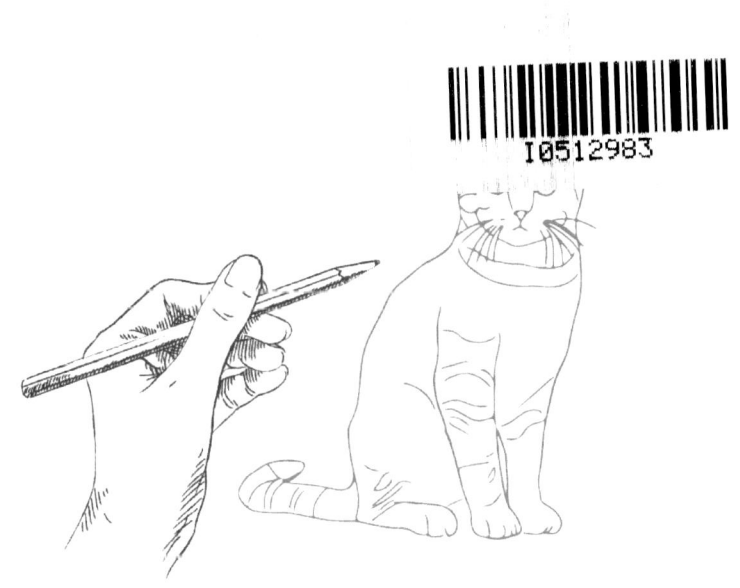

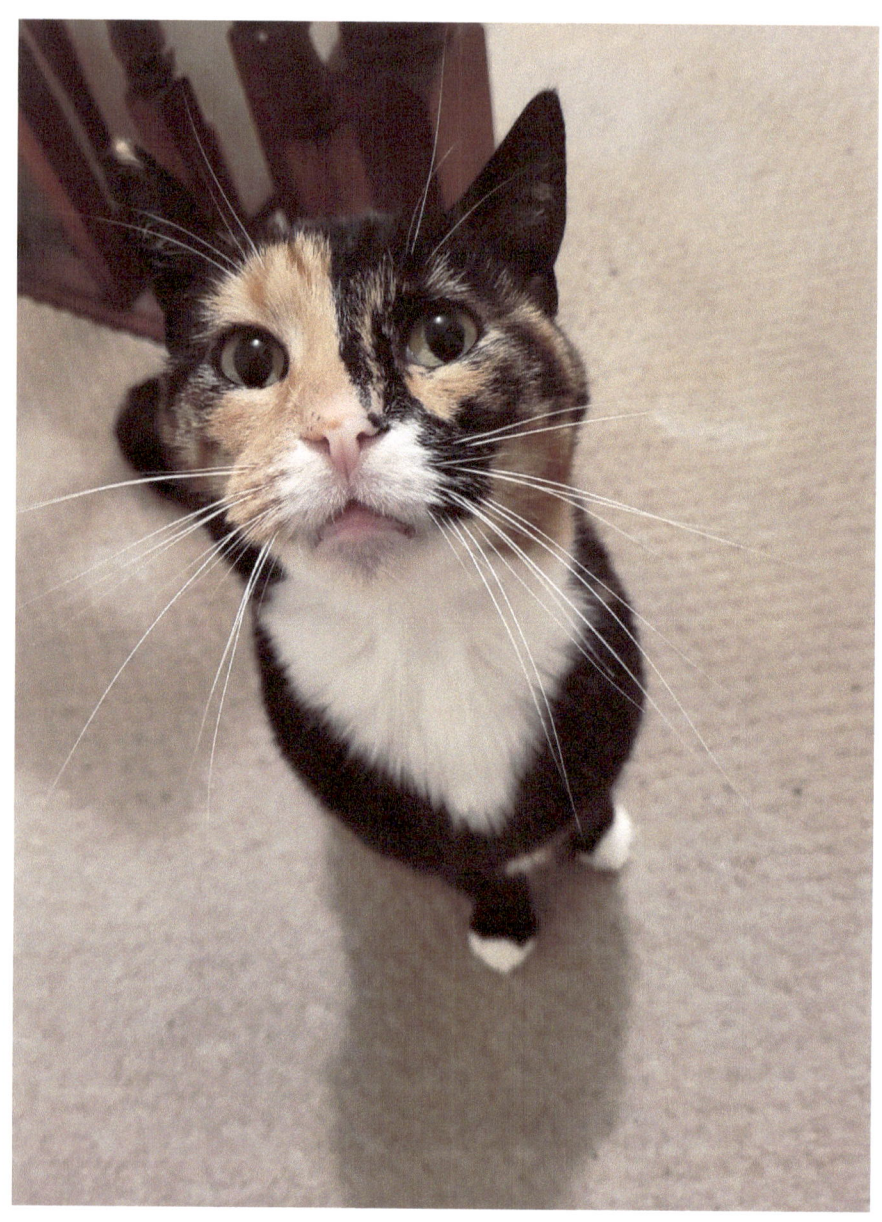

Draw Mia, the cat

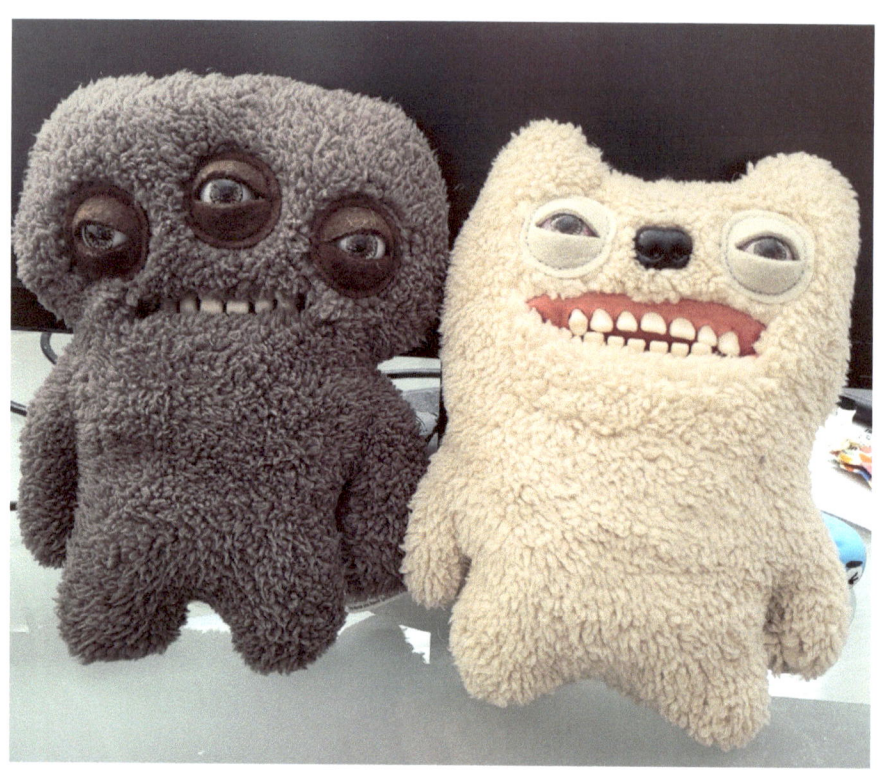

Draw the Fugglers

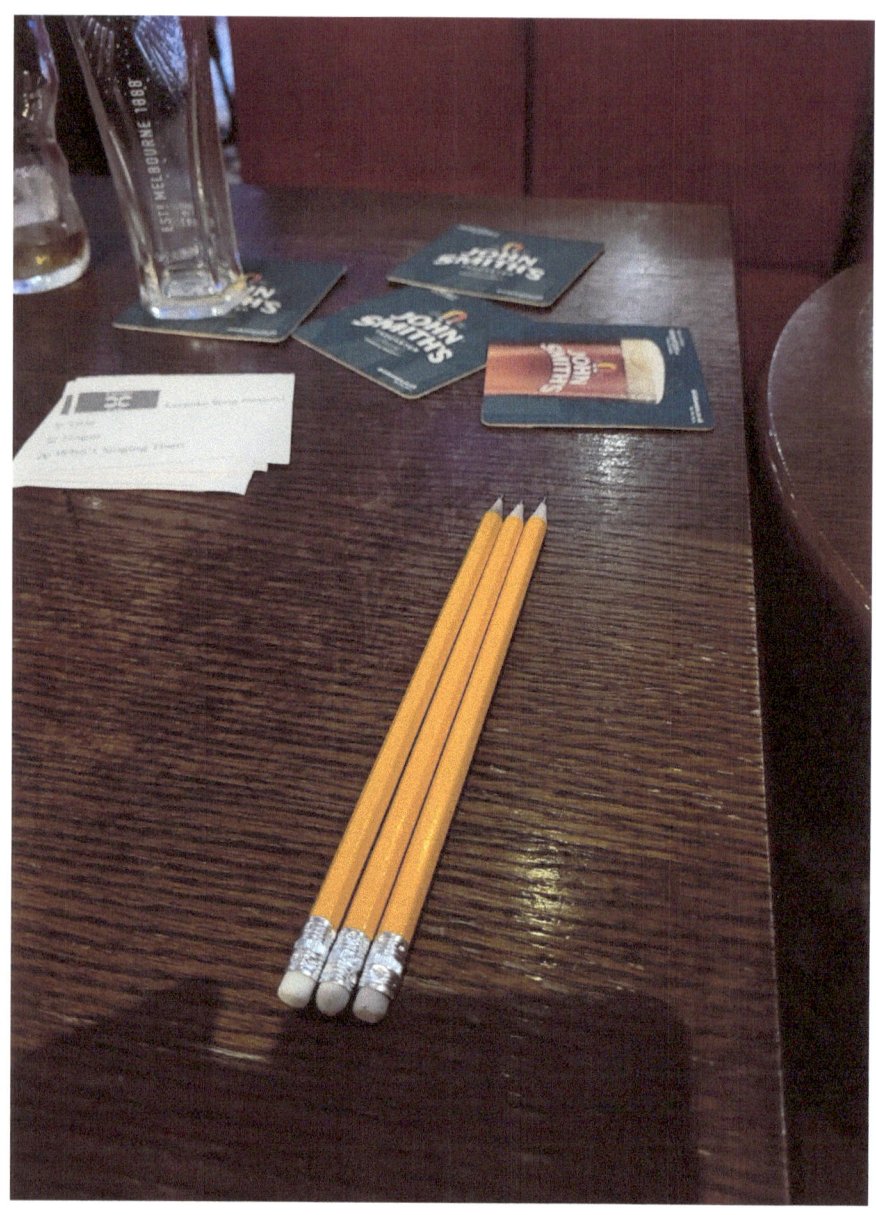

Draw pencils on a table

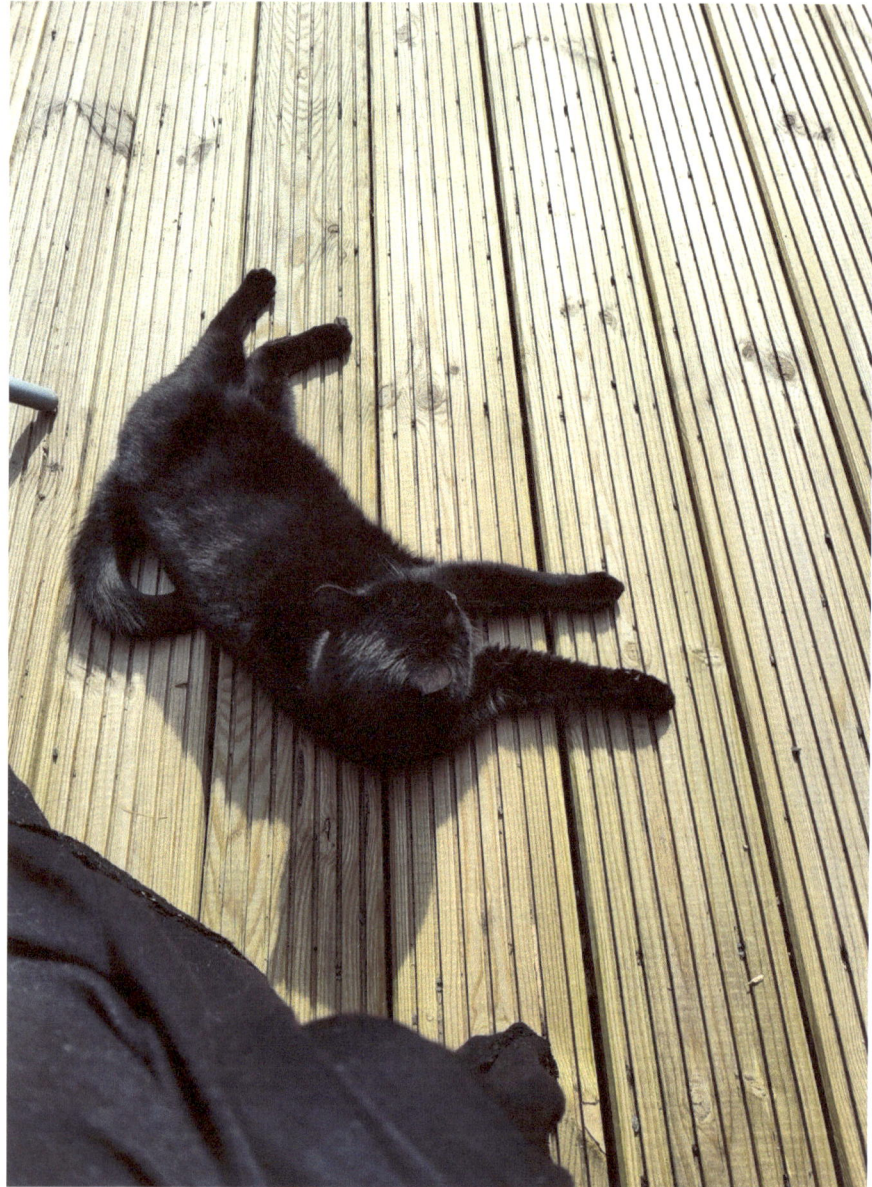

Draw Dave, the cat

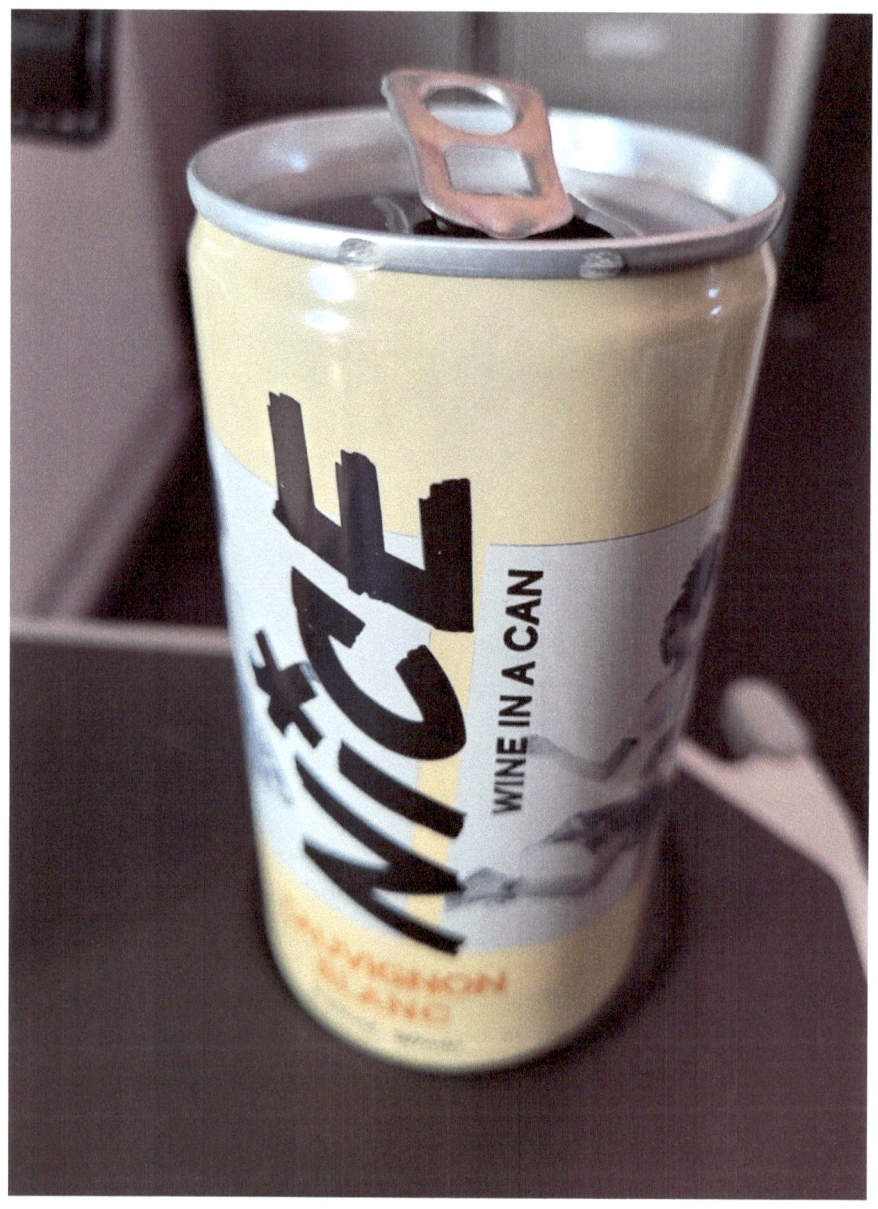

Draw a can of wine (courtesy Virgin Atlantic Airlines)

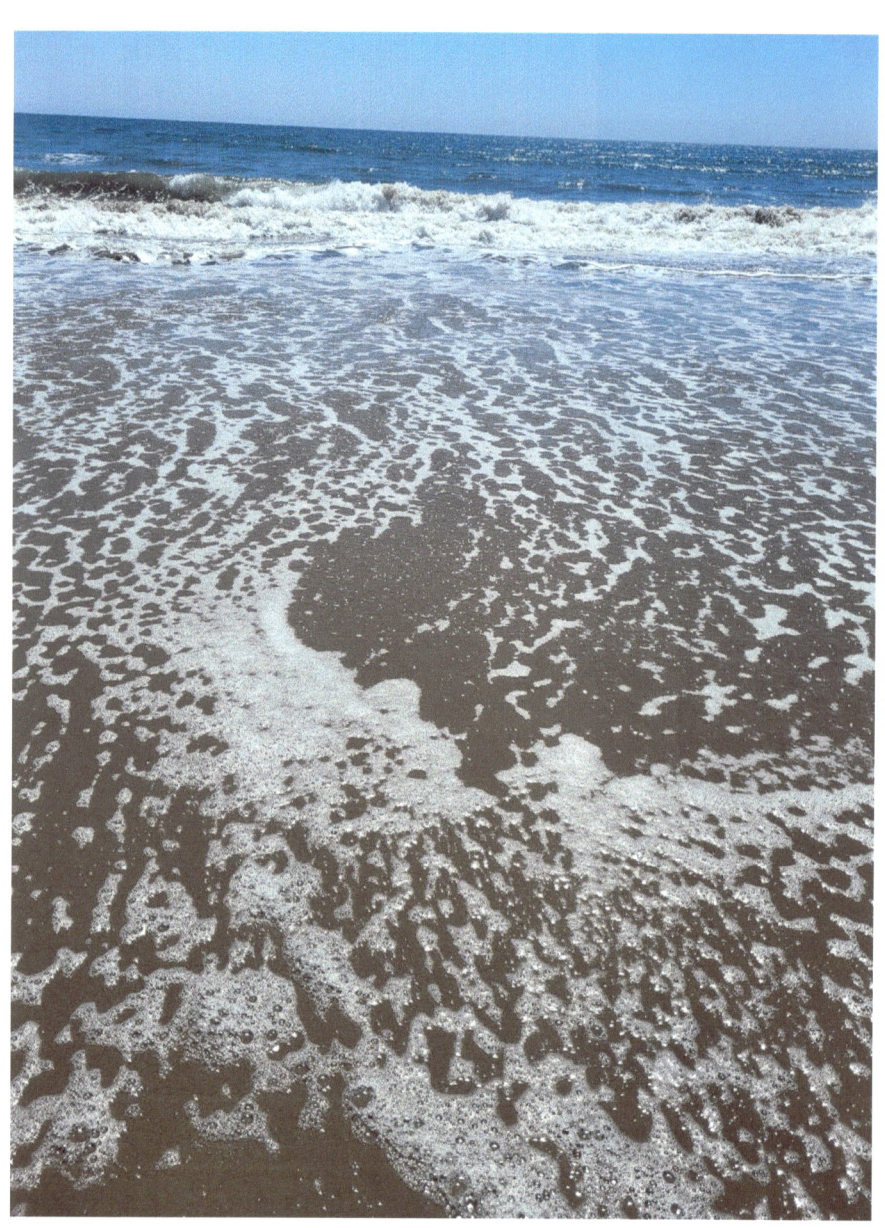

Draw a California beach

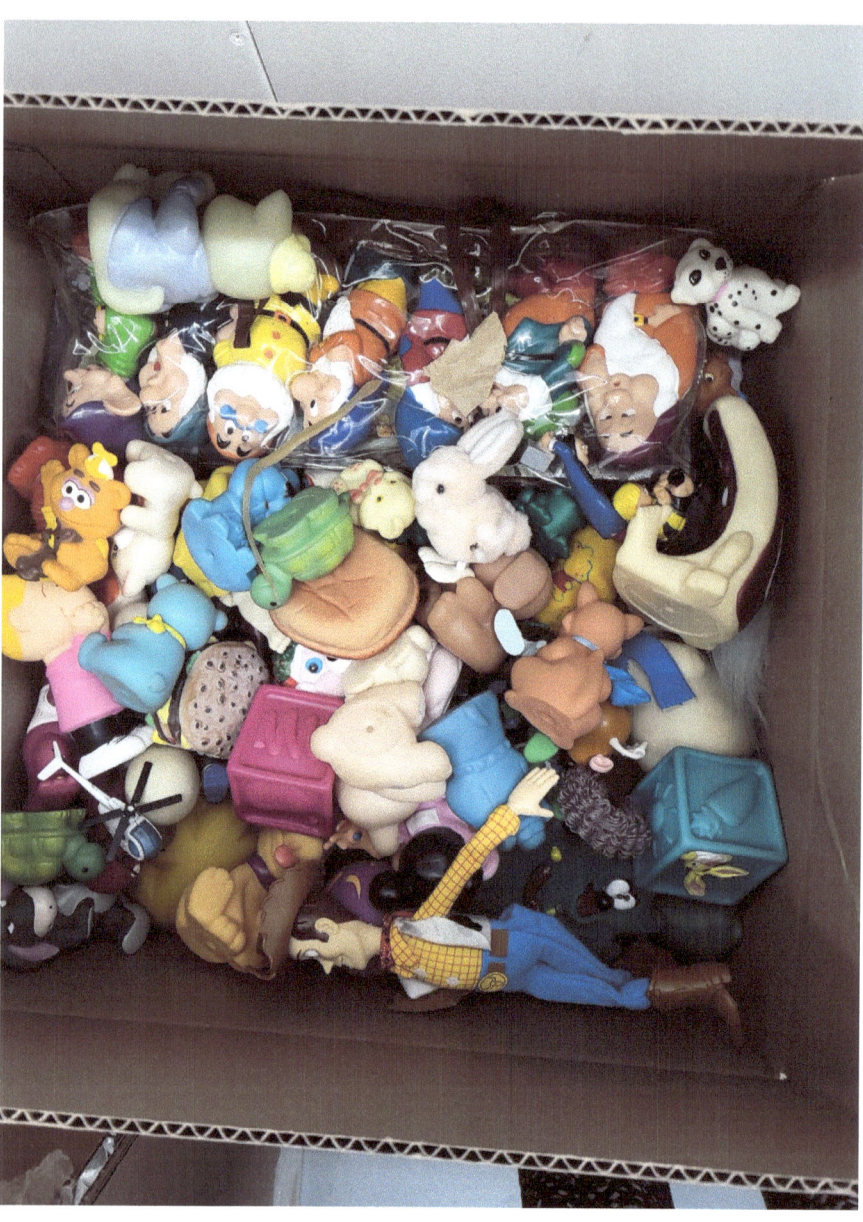

Draw a box full of toys

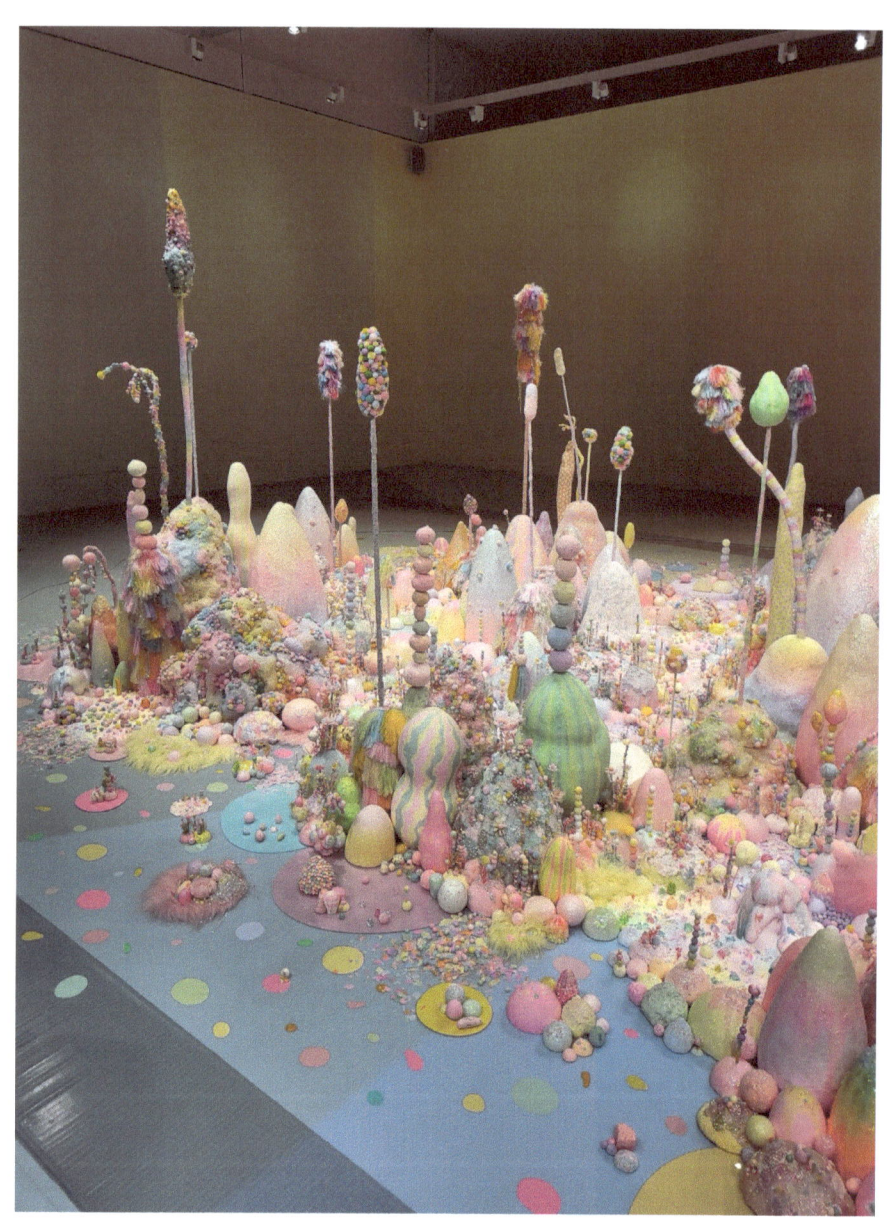

Draw an unusual art installation

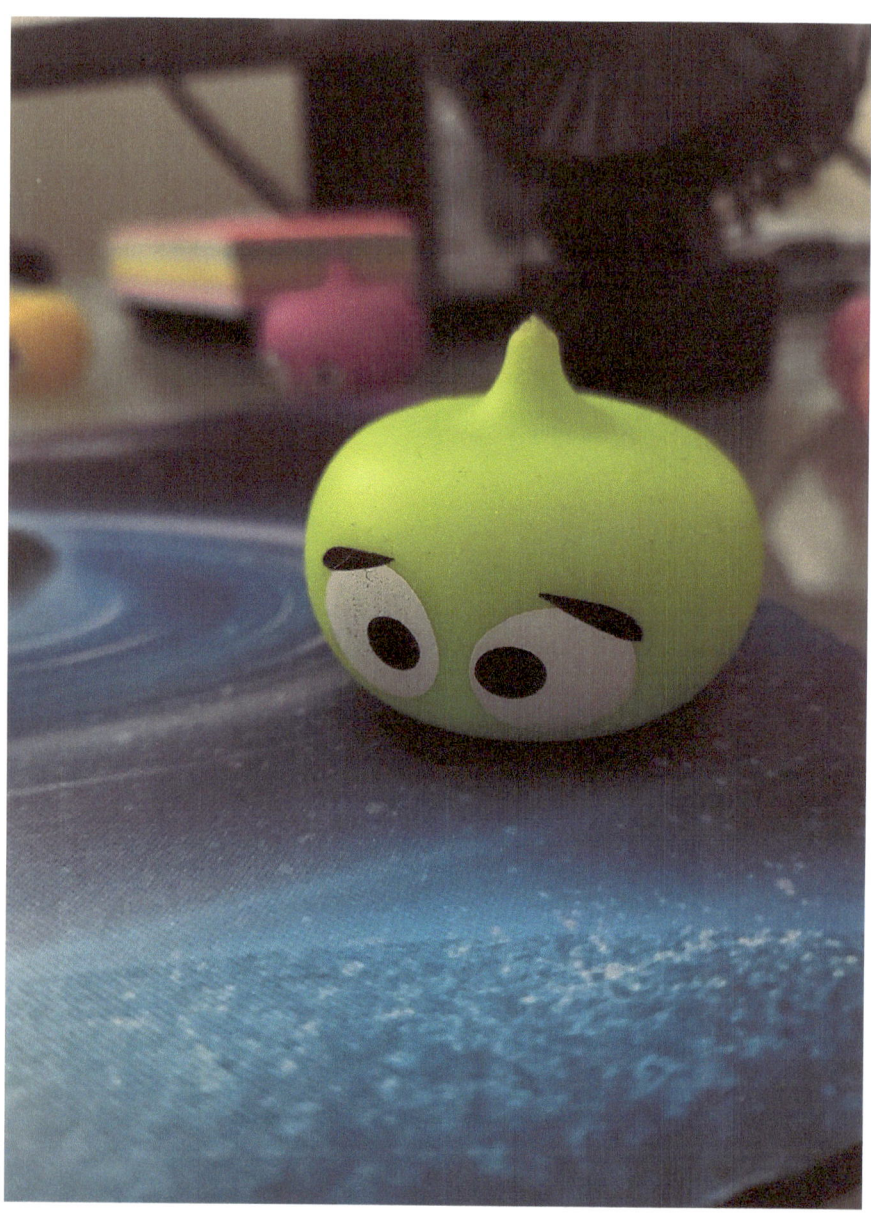

Draw a squeezy head

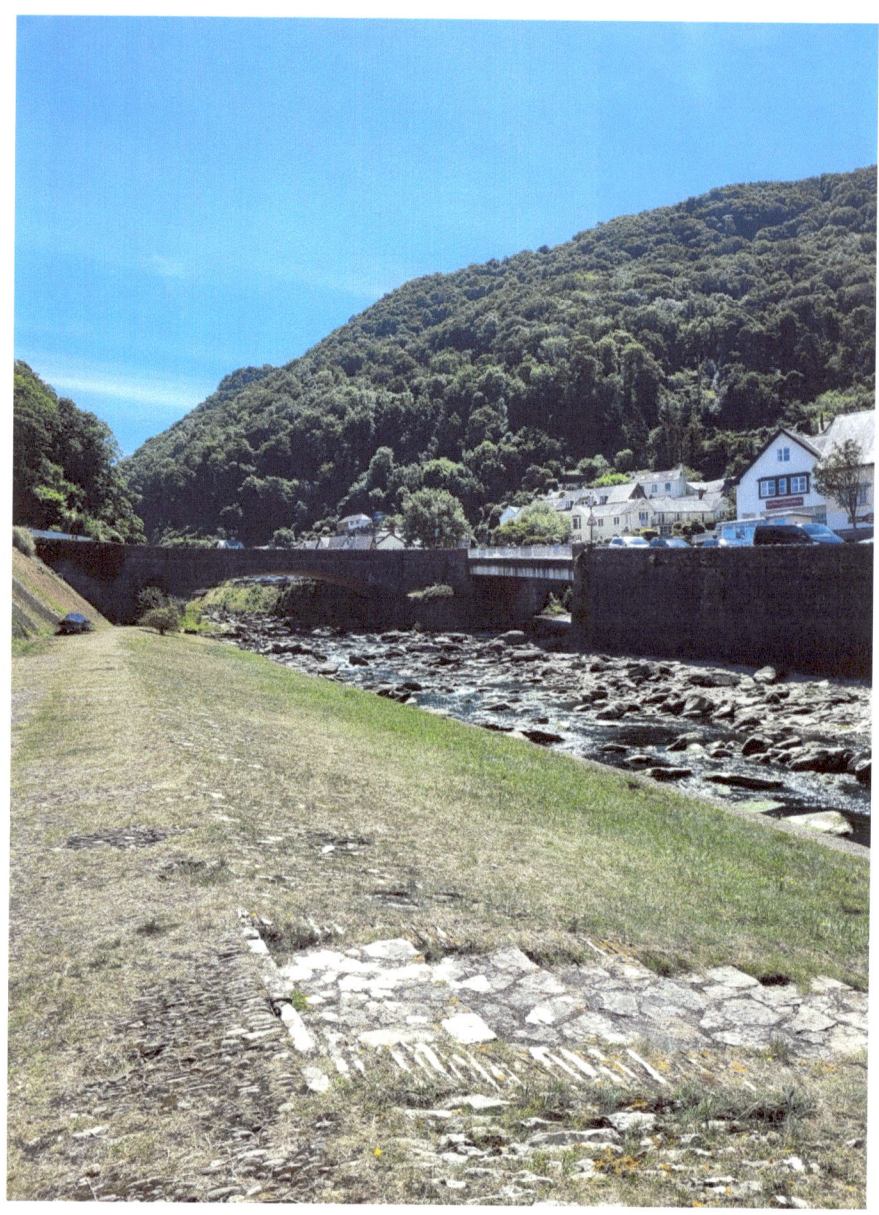

Draw a scenic view in Lynmouth, Devon, UK

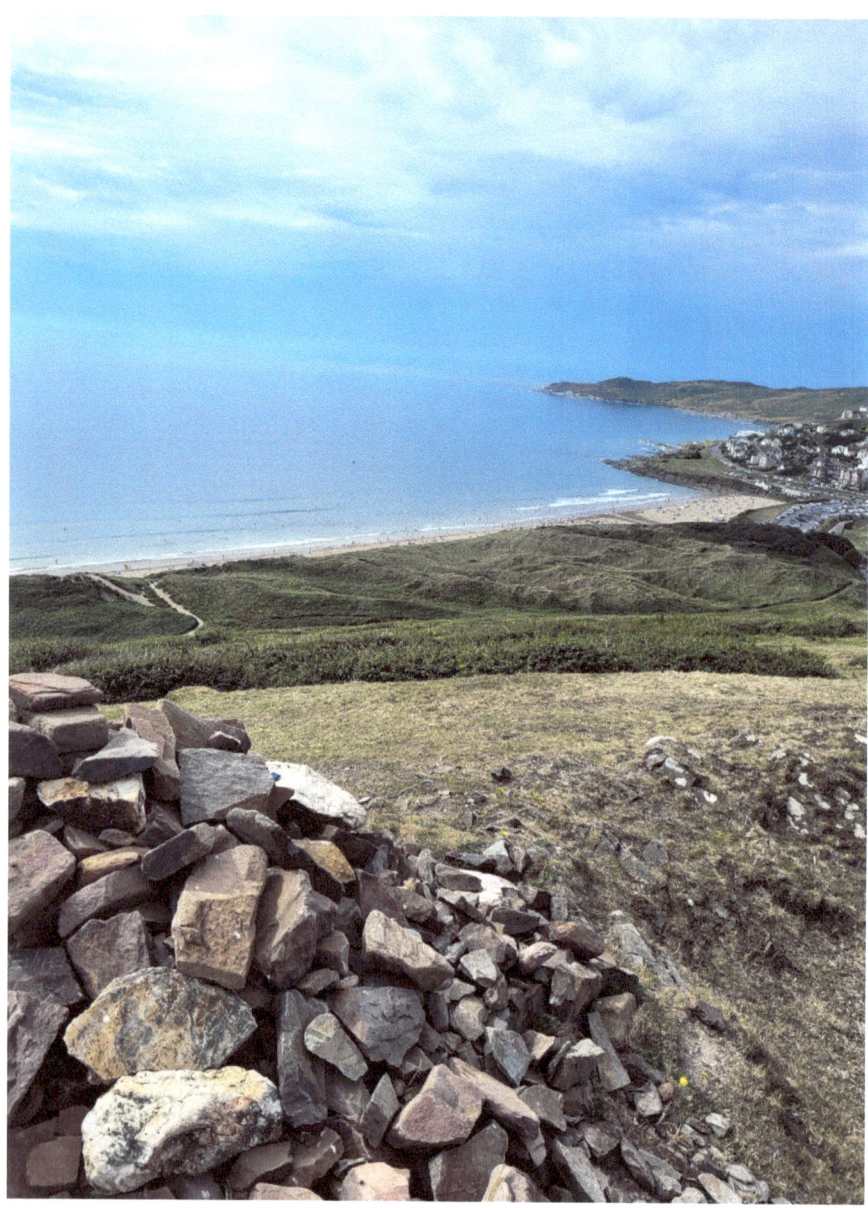

Draw a scenic view at Woolacombe Beach, Devon, UK

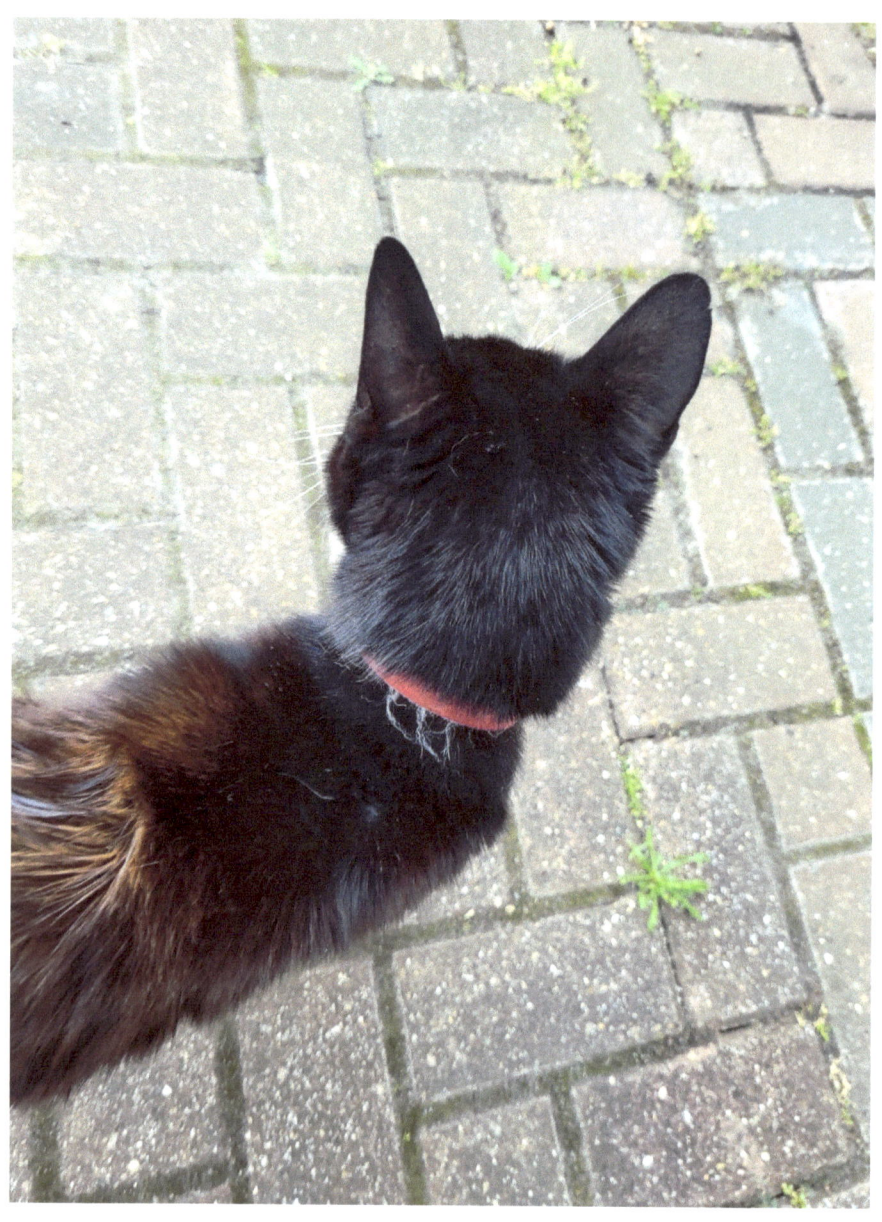

Draw Socks, the cat

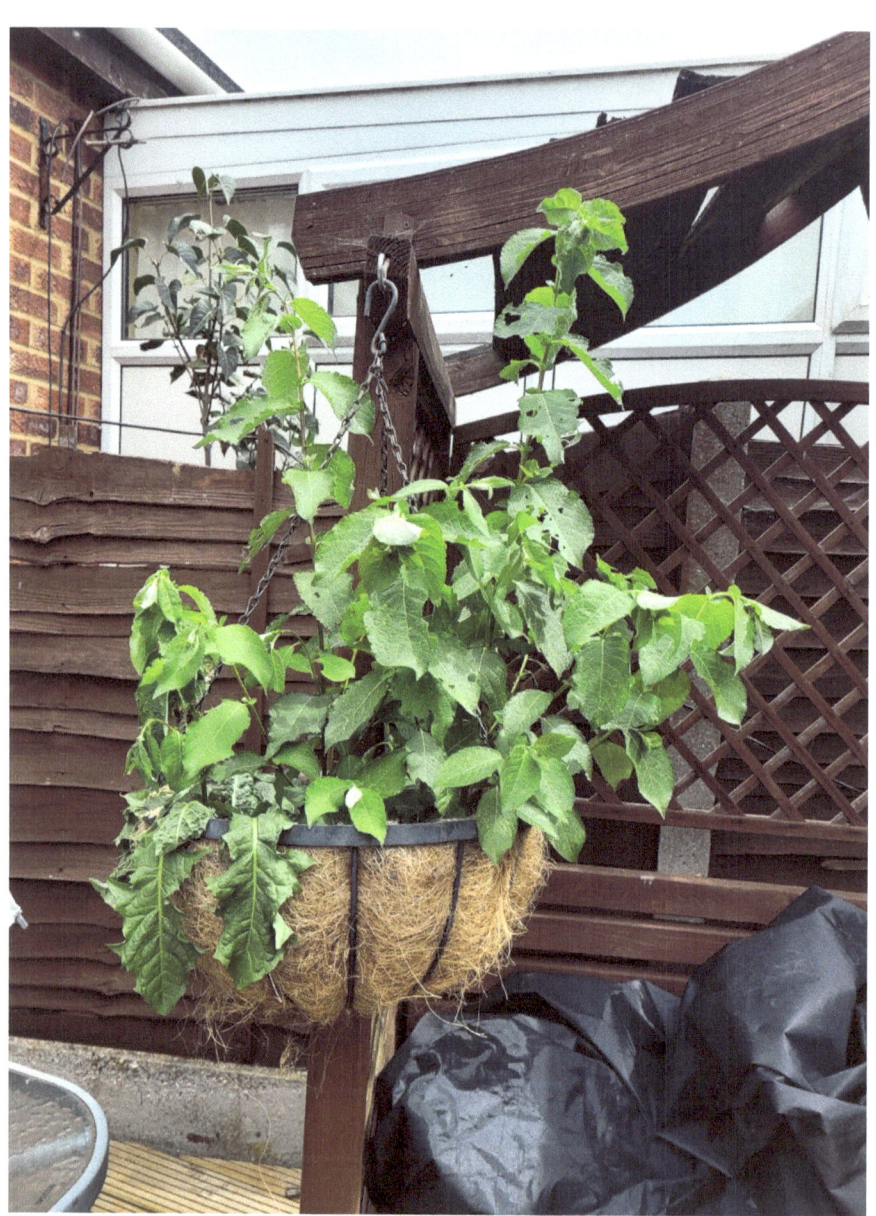

Draw a picture of an unidentified plant

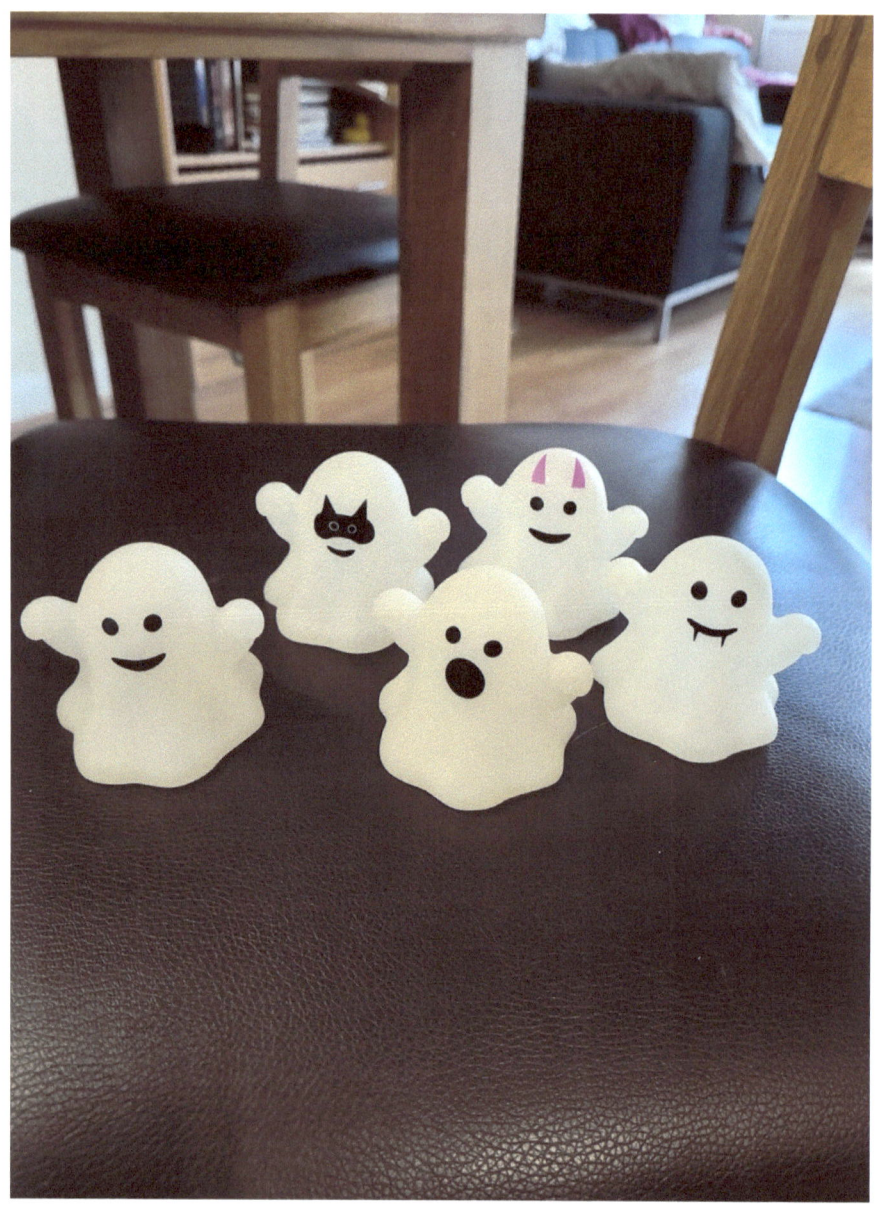

Draw a picture of some cute ghost toys

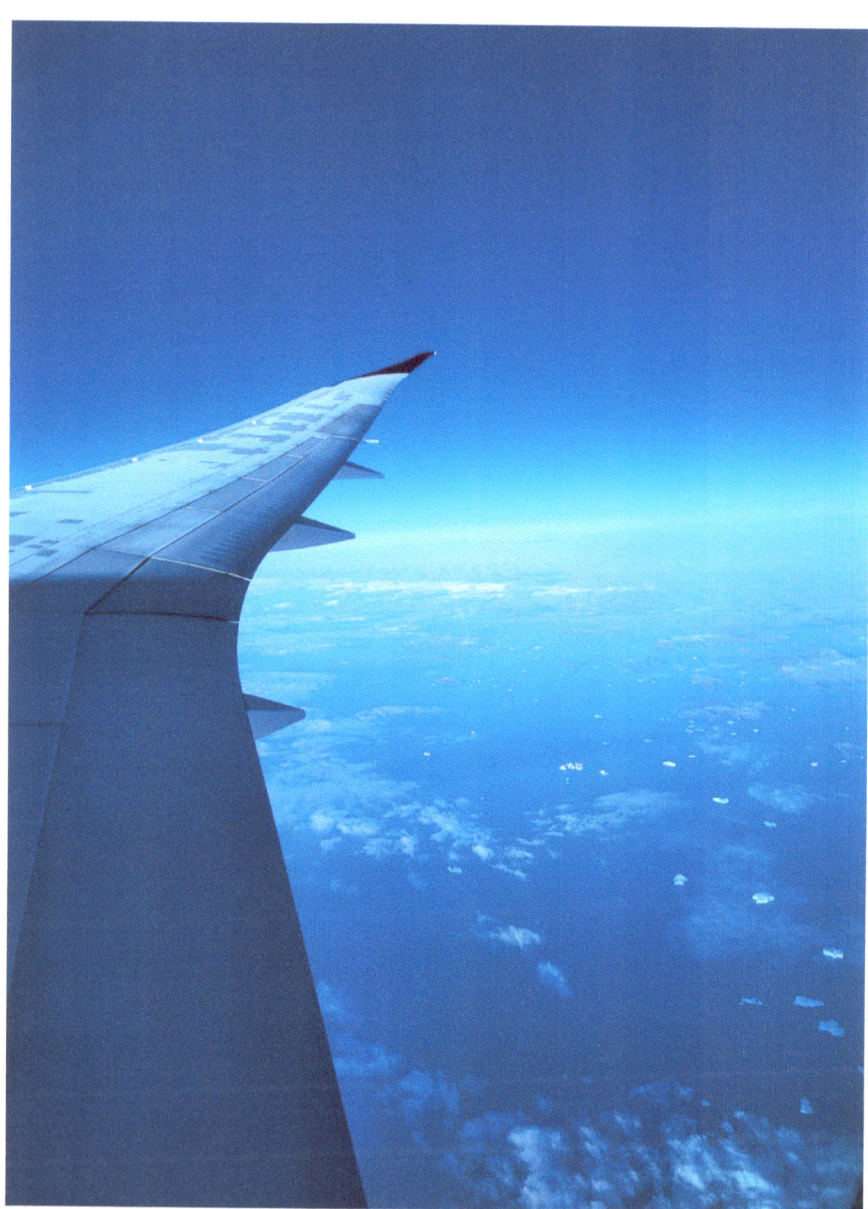

Draw a picture of the view from an airplane

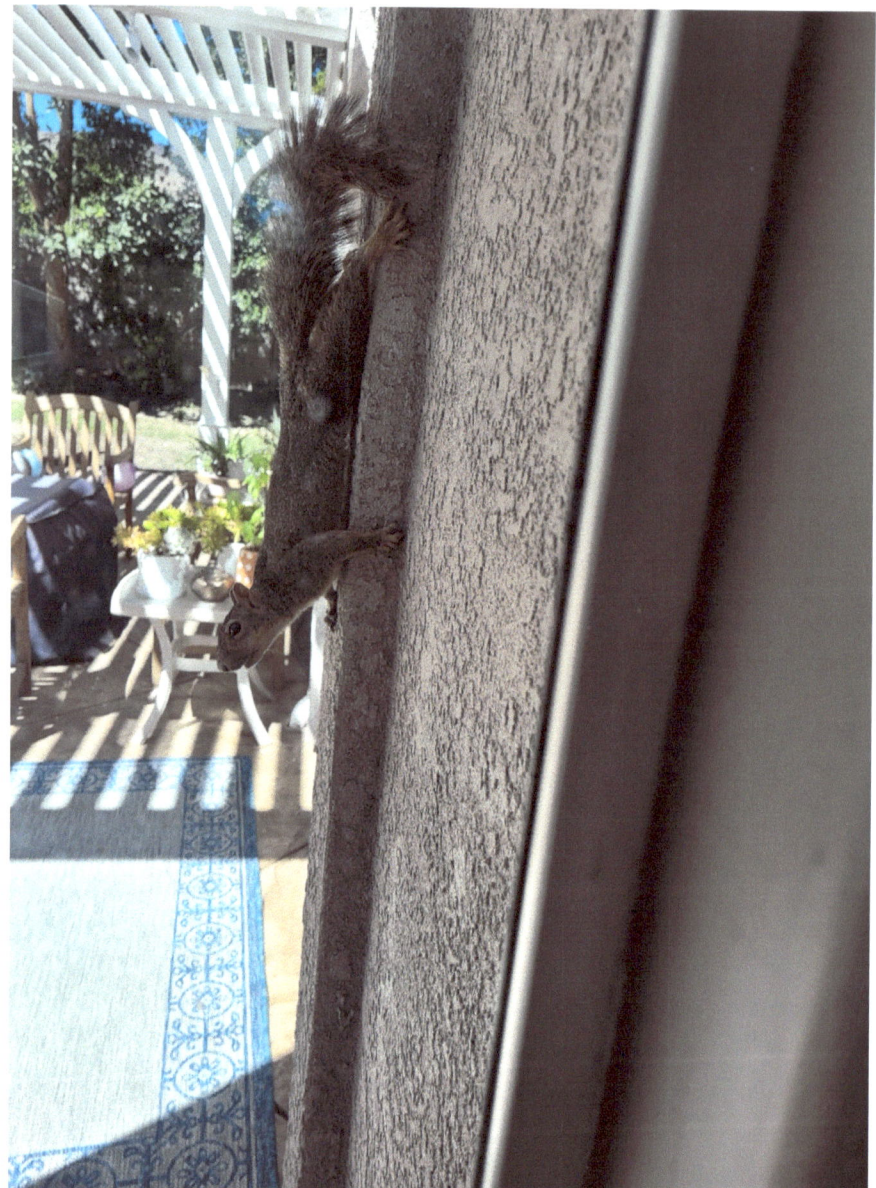

Draw a picture of a squirrel on a wall

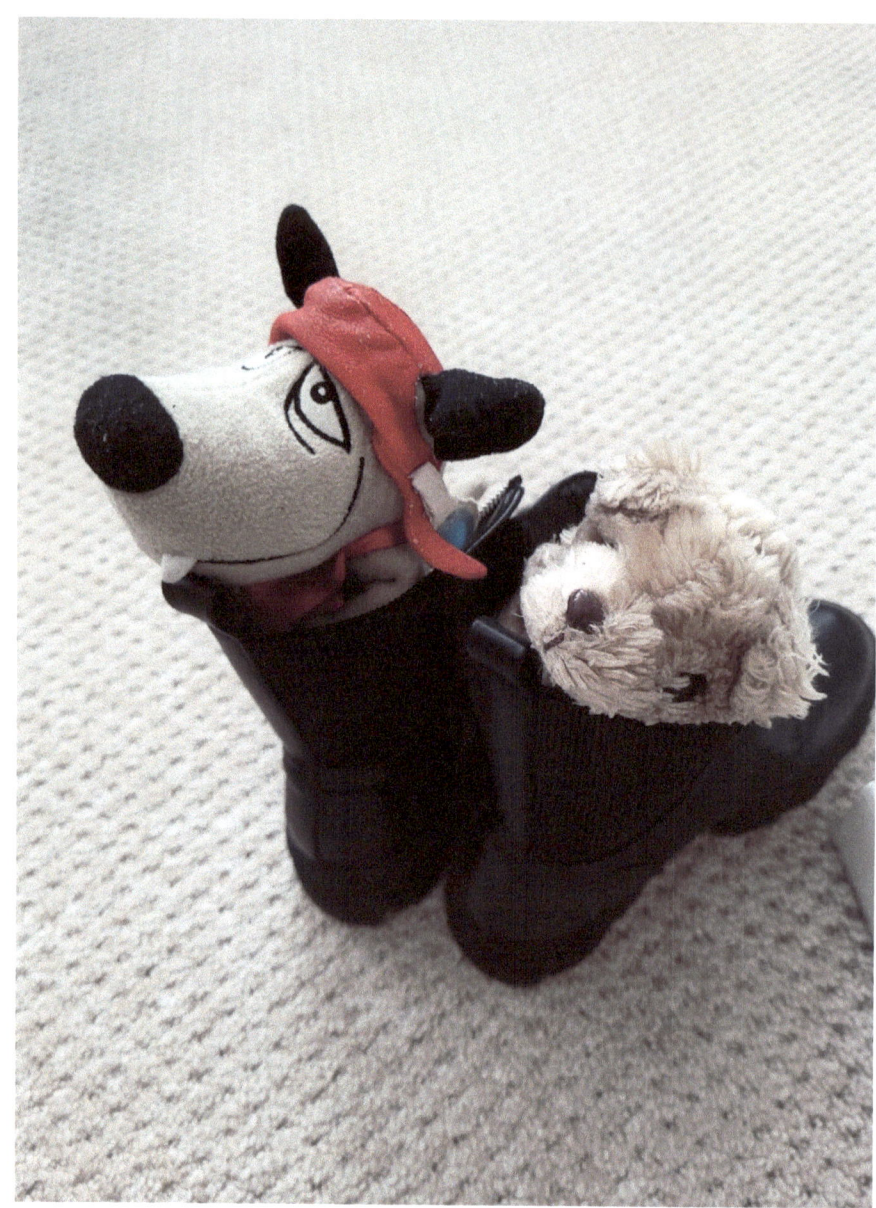

Draw a picture of stuffed toys sitting in my boots

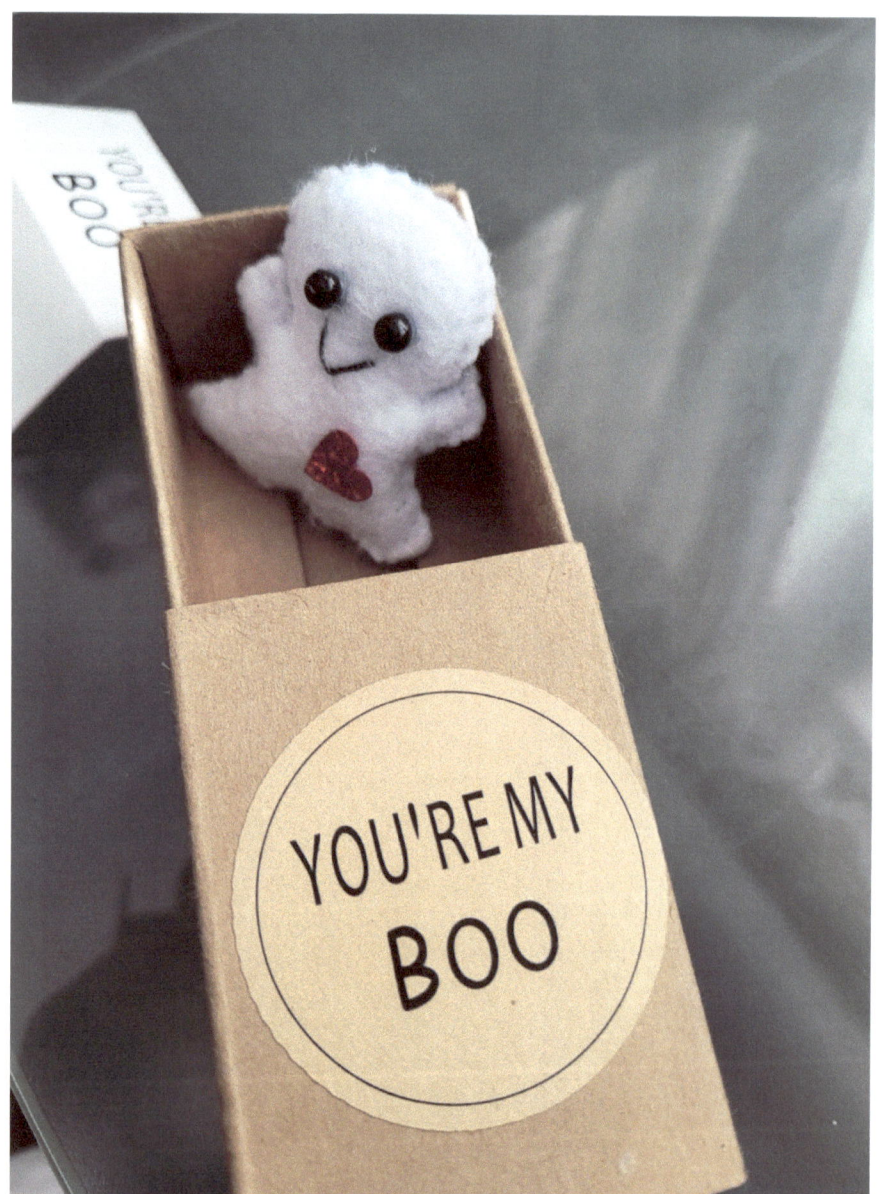

Draw a picture of a ghost in a box

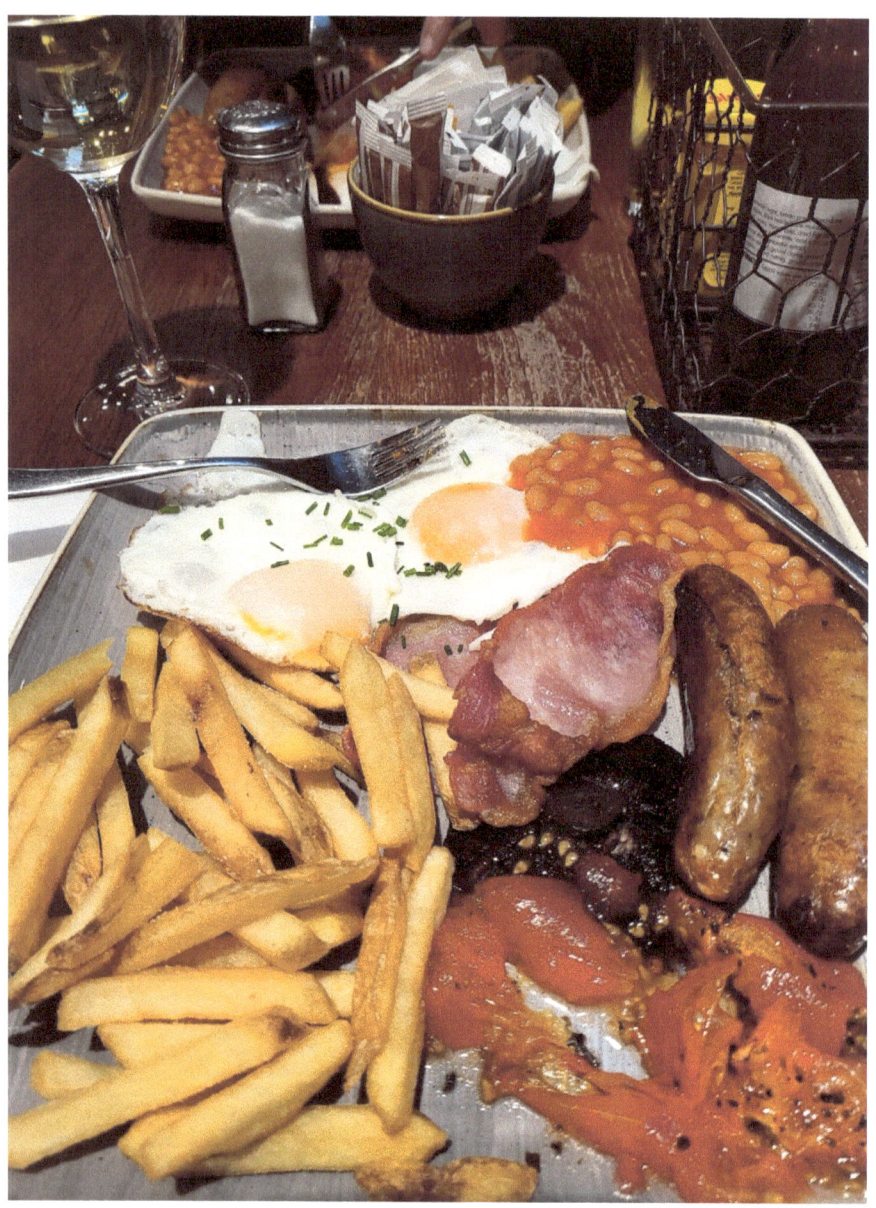

Draw a picture of an English breakfast

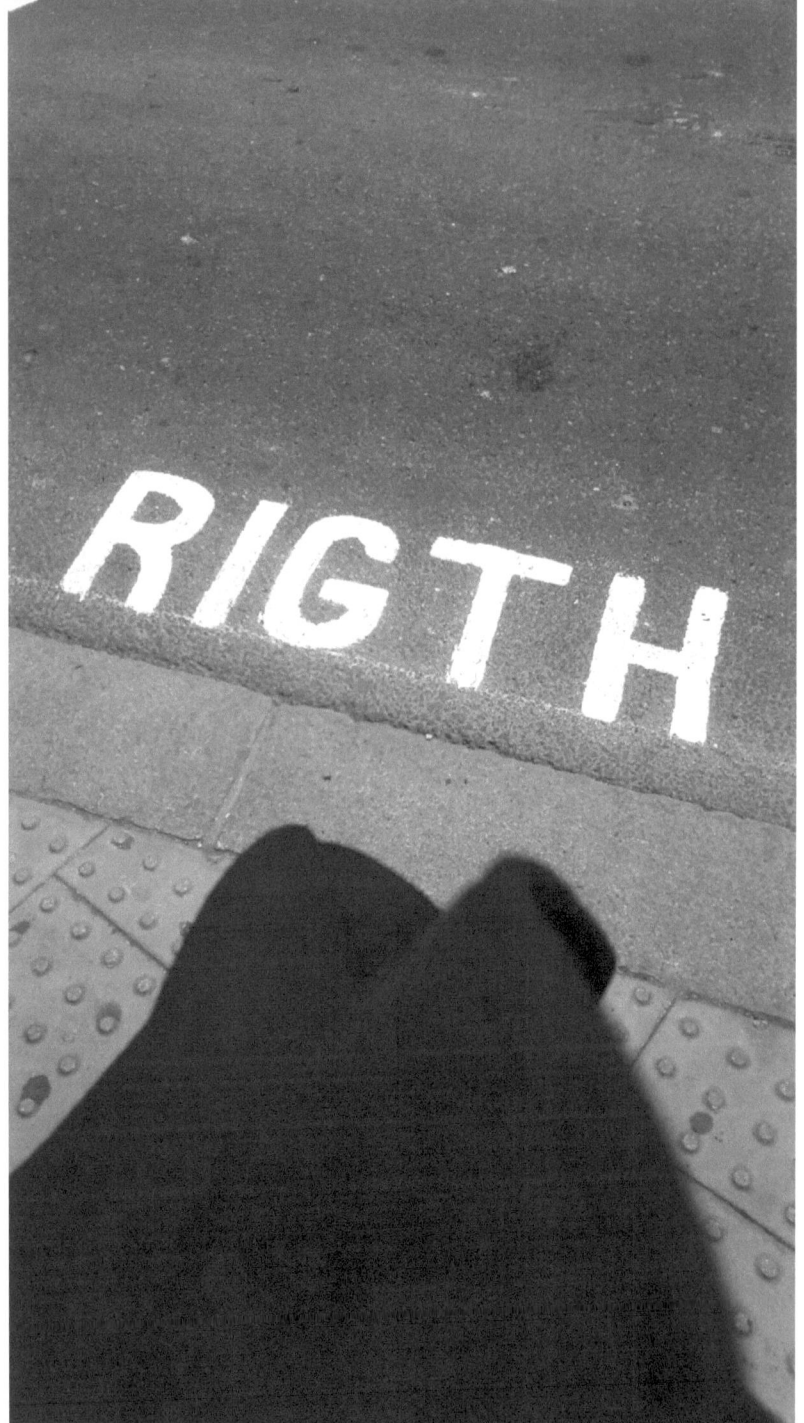

Draw a picture of a London street typo

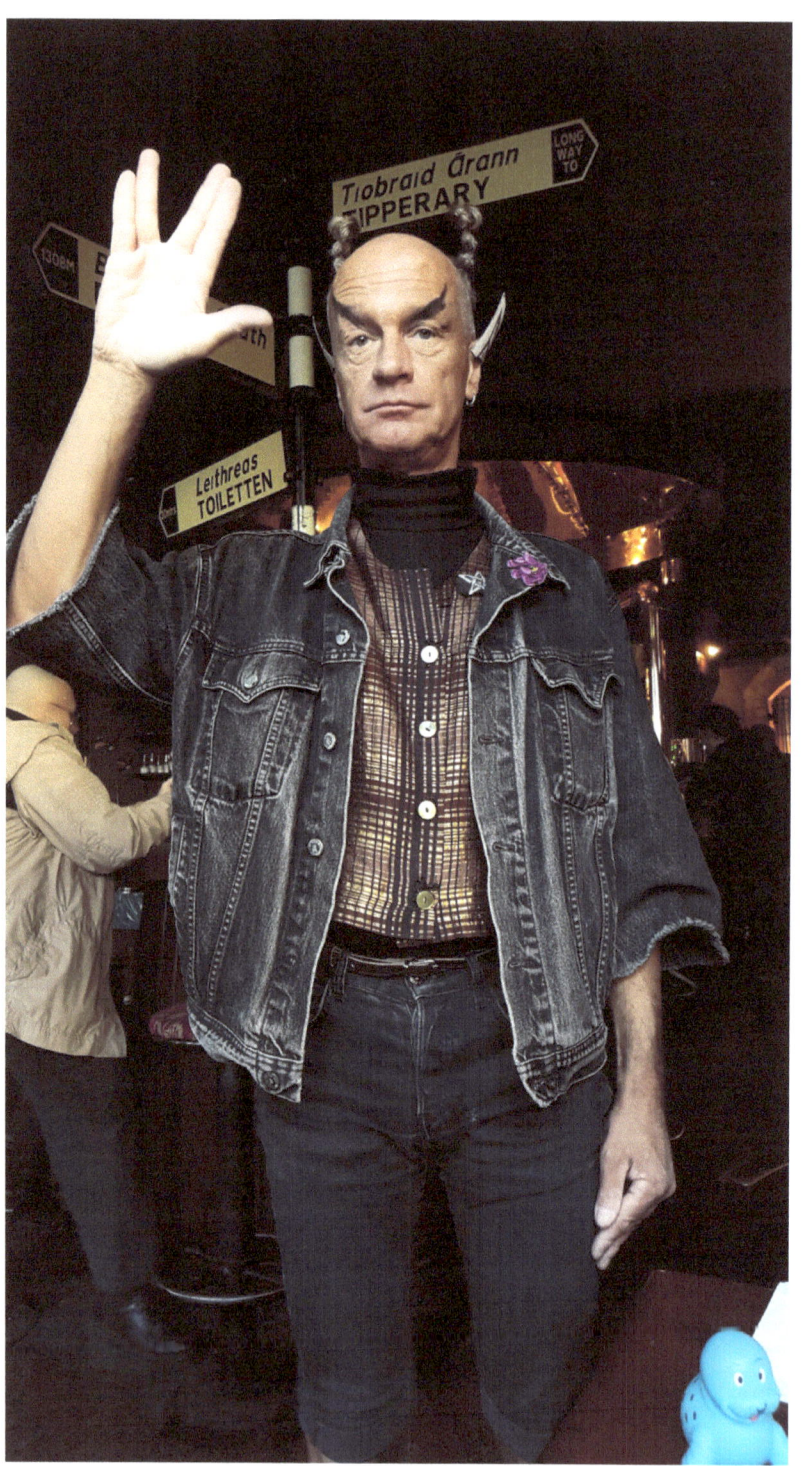

Draw a picture of Jurjen (R.I.P.)

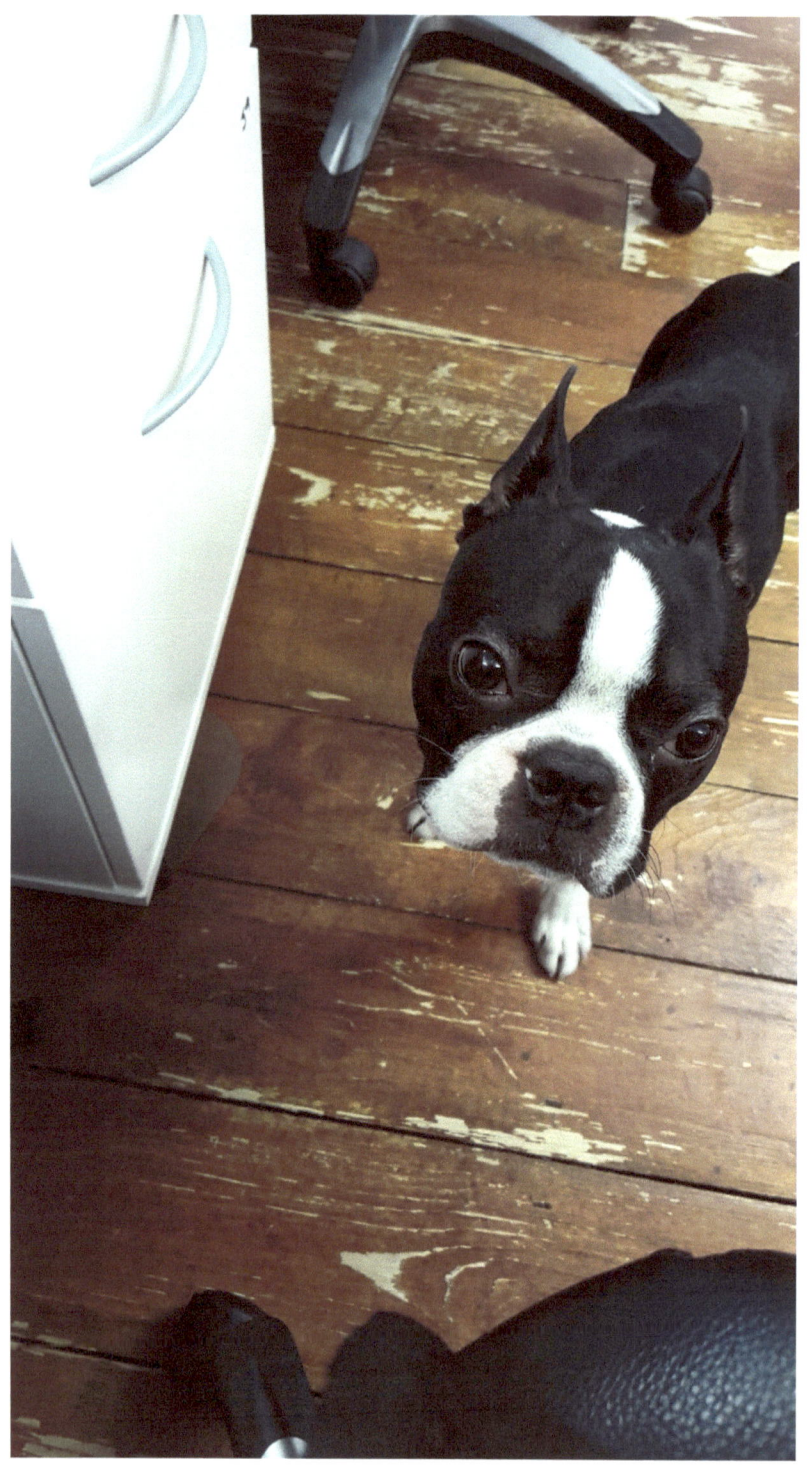

Draw a picture of an office dog

www.ingramcontent.com/pod-product-compliance
Lightning Source LLC
Chambersburg PA
CBHW061616230526
45473CB00031BA/2656